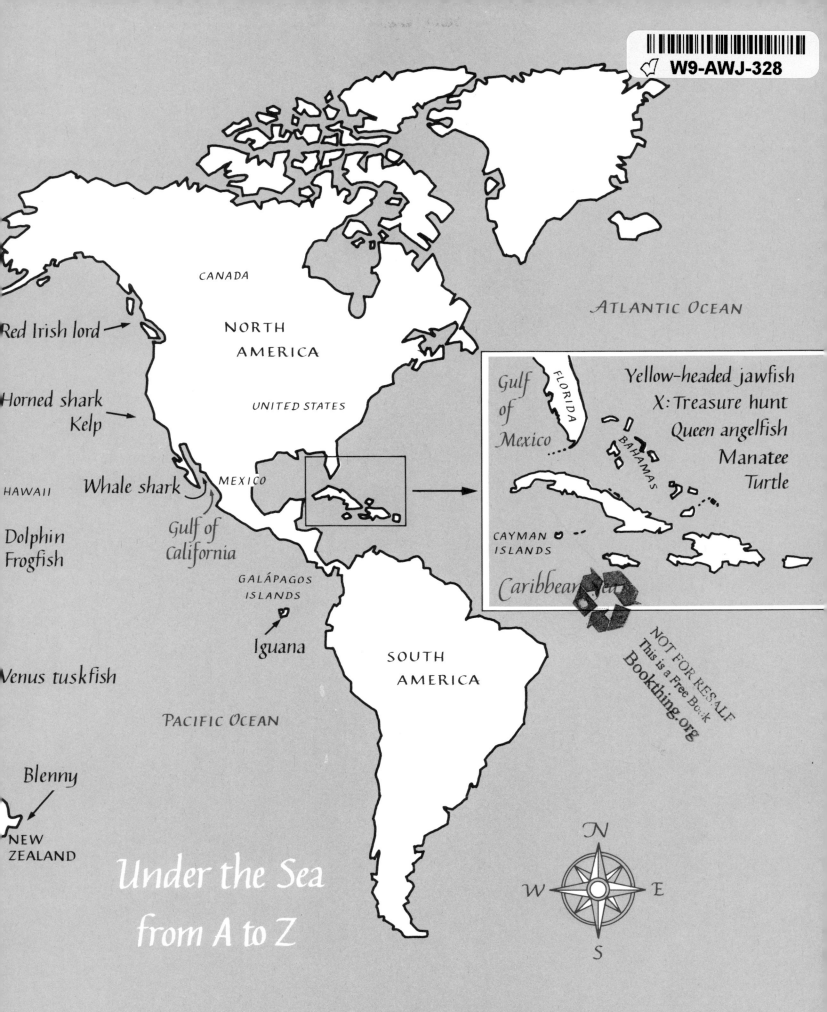

W9-AWJ-328

CANADA

NORTH
AMERICA

ATLANTIC OCEAN

Red Irish lord →

UNITED STATES

Horned shark
Kelp →

HAWAII    Whale shark    MEXICO

Dolphin
Frogfish

Gulf of
California

GALÁPAGOS
ISLANDS

Iguana

SOUTH
AMERICA

Venus tuskfish

PACIFIC OCEAN

Blenny

NEW
ZEALAND

Gulf
of
Mexico

FLORIDA

Yellow-headed jawfish
X: Treasure hunt
Queen angelfish
Manatee
Turtle

BAHAMAS

CAYMAN
ISLANDS

Caribbean Sea

NOT FOR RESALE
This is a Free Book
Bookthing.org

## Under the Sea
## from A to Z

N
W    E
S

© Claudia Carlson

# Under the Sea
# from A to Z

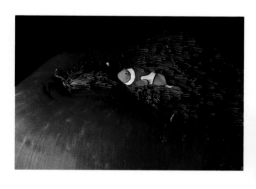

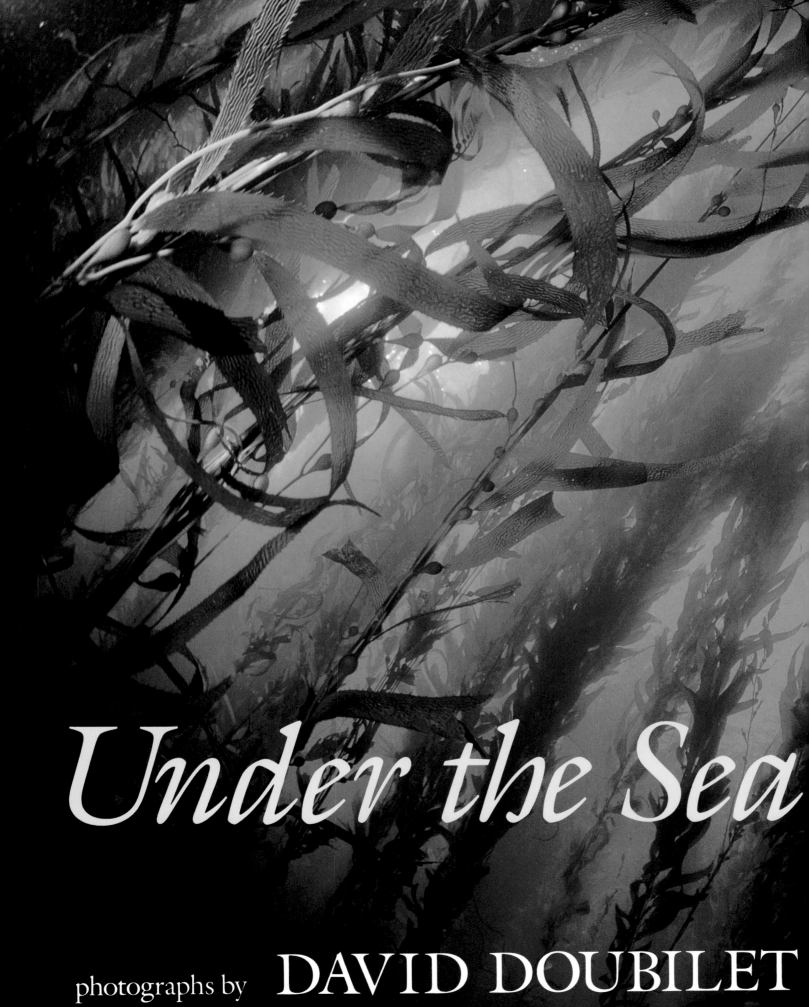

# *Under the Sea*

photographs by **DAVID DOUBILET**

# from A to Z
## by ANNE DOUBILET

Crown Publishers, Inc., New York

*For Emily*

Copyright © 1991 by Anne Doubilet and
David Doubilet.
All rights reserved. No part of this book may be
reproduced or transmitted in any form or by any
means, electronic or mechanical, including
photocopying, recording, or by any information
storage and retrieval system, without permission in
writing from the publisher.
Published by Crown Publishers, Inc., a Random
House company, 225 Park Avenue South, New
York, New York 10003
CROWN is a trademark of Crown Publishers, Inc.

Map by Claudia Carlson
Manufactured in Japan

Library of Congress Cataloging-in-Publication
Data
Doubilet, Anne.
  Under the Sea from A to Z / text by Anne
Doubilet; photos by David Doubilet.
      p.   cm. Summary: Presents photographs of
exotic marine life from A to Z. 1. Marine fauna—
Juvenile literature.   2. Marine flora—Juvenile
literature.   3. English language—Alphabet—
Juvenile literature.   [1.   Marine animals.
2. Marine plants.   3. Alphabet.]   I. Doubilet,
David.   II. Title.
QL122.2.D68   1991      591.92—dc20      [E]
                                                              90-1355

ISBN 0-517-57836-0 (trade)
         0-517-57837-9 (lib. bdg.)

10  9  8  7  6  5  4  3  2  1

First Edition

Although they look like plants, anemones are animals. They live on rocks and with corals throughout the oceans of the world. They feed on anything that falls into the grasp of their tentacles, where stinging cells are located. In the Pacific Ocean, Indian Ocean, and Red Sea anemones live together with beautifully colored clownfish like this one. The clownfish is protected from predators within the anemone's stinging tentacles. In return it helps keep the anemone clean and drives away other fish that could harm the anemone. A sticky substance called mucus is made by the anemone to prevent it from stinging itself. The clownfish does not get stung because it rubs the mucus from the anemone on its body.

**Anemone**   Bismarck Sea, New Guinea

# A

# Some Anemones live with beautifully colored clownfish.

# This Blenny is only the size of your fingernail.

B

**Crested blenny**   Pacific Ocean, New Zealand

Blennies are usually tiny. Most are only the size of your fingernail, although some species grow up to eight feet long. This small blenny lives in a hole in the rock surrounded by pink and orange anemones. It eats plankton that drifts by in the current, but quickly pulls back into its safe home when something big swims by. Plankton is a kind of thick soup of the sea made up of microscopic plants, fish eggs, and creatures such as baby fish, tiny crabs, and tiny shrimps. For such a small creature the blenny has enormous, colorful eyes that enable it to see the food it eats in the dark water.

The giant spider crab is the largest crab in the world. The males can measure up to twelve feet from claw tip to claw tip. For most of the year giant spider crabs live in the cold, deep waters off Japan's coast, but in the spring they migrate up to shallow water to mate and lay eggs. They have tiny brains for such large bodies. It takes a long time for the brain to send a message to the claws, and so the crab moves very slowly in its dark, deep ocean world. Giant spider crabs are rare, and the Japanese value them highly. When they find the crab's shells, they paint faces on them and keep them as good-luck charms.

**Giant spider crab**  Pacific Ocean, Japan

# This Crab
# measures twelve feet
# from claw to claw.

# D

## The shape of a Dolphin's jaw makes it look as though it is smiling.

This bottlenose dolphin seems to have a friendly, smiling face. While it is the natural shape of their jaws that makes it look as though they are always smiling, dolphins, which have large brains, can form strong attachments to people. The bottlenose dolphin grows up to thirteen feet long and 650 pounds in weight. It has two rows of strong, sharp teeth and eats fish. It dives deep in the sea, but, like humans, dolphins are air-breathing mammals and must come to the surface regularly to breathe. Dolphins make high-pitched squeaks and clicks that bounce, or echo, off other objects in the sea. By listening to the echoes, dolphins can find where they are and find their food. This is called echolocation. Other kinds of clicks and squeaks are made by dolphins to communicate with each other.

**Bottlenose dolphin**   Pacific Ocean, Hawaii

**White moray eel**   Red Sea, Sinai Peninsula, Egypt

These three white moray eels are crowded together in one small coral hole. They are small and thin, about one foot in length and about as round as a hot dog. Larger green moray eels can grow to be eight feet long. Because they have gills inside their throats—instead of outside, like other fish—moray eels are constantly opening and closing their mouths to breathe. This makes them look scary and ferocious. But they will not attack, unless a diver sticks a hand in their home. Moray eels leave their coral holes at night to hunt for fish, crabs, lobsters, and octopuses.

# These three Eels are crowded together in one small hole.

# The Frogfish uses its unusual fins to hop around in coral trees.

F

**Yellow frogfish**   Pacific Ocean, Hawaii

The yellow frogfish has unusual pectoral fins. They are more like arms—complete with elbows! The frogfish uses them to hop around in coral trees or on the ocean bottom. This one is living on a large black coral tree. About the size of a tennis ball, the frogfish is also known as an anglerfish. It has a tiny "fishing line" on the top of its head with a small piece of flesh on the end that looks like bait. Waving around in the water, the bait attracts other fish; those who venture too close are quickly gobbled up by the frogfish.

# G

## Good camouflage protects this Goby from hungry predators.

**Whip coral goby**   Bismarck Sea, New Guinea

This goby is only the length of a toothpick and feeds on tiny plankton that drifts by in the ocean currents. Other species of goby grow up to a foot in length. Because its body is clear and its eyes and internal organs are red, this goby blends in perfectly with the stalk of red coral upon which it is perched. It will spend its entire life on the red coral, where its camouflage protects it from hungry predators.

# Horned Sharks have special teeth for grinding up food.

H

**Horned shark**  Pacific Ocean, California

Also known as the pig shark, the horned shark is a bottom dweller. It does not swim in the deep waters of the open ocean like other sharks, but lies around on the bottom in the shallower waters close to shore. It feeds on other creatures that live on the bottom, such as clams and oysters. Also unlike other sharks, a horned shark has different kinds of teeth in both upper and lower jaws. The front teeth are used for grasping and holding its food; the back teeth act as very strong grinders. Horned sharks can grow to a length of three feet.

# Marine Iguanas dive underwater to feed on algae.

The only species of marine, or saltwater, iguana in the world lives in the Galápagos Islands in the Pacific Ocean. Because the Galápagos Islands are so isolated from other land masses—they are 600 miles off the coast of Ecuador in South America—many unique forms of wildlife have developed there and nowhere else on earth. The marine iguana spends most of its time on the islands' black volcanic rocks soaking up the sun because, like most reptiles and lizards, it is cold blooded and its body temperature depends on the temperature of the air around it. When hungry, it dives underwater to graze on the algae that carpet the rocky bottom. Almost one foot long, it swims slowly and clumsily and seems to use its long tail for steering.

**Marine iguana**   Pacific Ocean, Galápagos Islands

 This Jellyfish has hundreds of stingers.

Looking like a collection of green and purple pipe cleaners, this Japanese cherry blossom jellyfish pulses slowly through the cold, dark waters off Japan's coast. It is small, about the size of a Ping-Pong ball. Each purple-tipped tentacle has hundreds of stinging cells that paralyze its prey. Because the jellyfish is clear, its internal organs are visible, and it glows like a jewel in the light from the photographer's flash. The red and yellow pouch in the middle is its stomach.

**Japanese cherry blossom jellyfish**
Pacific Ocean, Japan

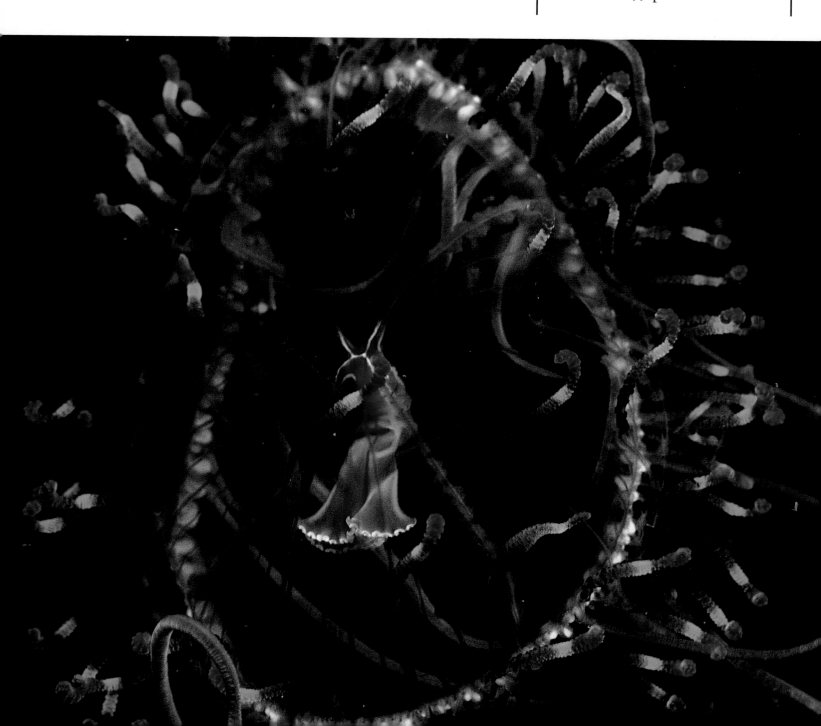

**Kelp**   Pacific Ocean, California

Kelp is a giant seaweed that grows in great forests in cool waters throughout the world. The largest and most beautiful kelp forests are off the California coast in the North Pacific Ocean, where individual kelp plants can grow up to one hundred feet high. Each plant is made up of leaves, a wiry stalk, a bulblike float, and a holdfast, which anchors the stalk to the bottom. Living within the kelp forest are seals, sea otters, and schools of fish. Snails and sea urchins eat kelp. Small fish graze on plankton that dusts the surface of the kelp leaves. As well as providing food and protection for marine life, kelp is also a valuable natural resource. It is used in many products, including ice cream, face cream, paint, toothpaste, and fertilizer.

# Kelp grows in great underwater forests.

# This Leafy Sea Dragon is carrying a baby on its back.

L

**Leafy sea dragon**
Great Australian Bight, Australia

The leafy sea dragon is a relative of the sea horse. It lives only in the cool, shallow waters off the South Australian coast. With its delicate, leaflike fins, it blends in with the seaweed and sea grass. It uses its long snout to suck up tiny marine creatures and small worms. Leafy sea dragons can grow up to one foot in length and, like sea horses, their skin is hard and bony. Look carefully at the photograph and you will see a well-camouflaged baby hitching a ride on its parent's back—a very rare sight.

Manatees belong to a group of mammals called sea cows that are closely related to elephants. They have elephant-like skin, and adults can weigh as much as 1,100 pounds. In the past, sailors and explorers who spotted them from a distance believed they were mermaids. This may be because of the graceful way they swim, or because female manatees lie on the surface of the water suckling their young against their chests. Manatees live in the Caribbean Sea, off Florida, and off the West African coast, where they eat sea grass and water plants. Sadly, the slow and gentle manatee is now an endangered species. Years ago sailors killed them for food. Today their homes are being destroyed by building, and many manatees have been run over by motorboats. This manatee is playing with the anchor rope of a motorboat.

**Manatee**   Gulf of Mexico, Florida

# Manatees
# are closely related
# to elephants.

# N

## This Nudibranch sways through the water like a belly dancer.

A nudibranch is like a snail without a shell. Instead of eyes, it has sensory horns and swims through the water or moves on the reef by sense of touch and smell. The name *nudibranch* (NEW-duh-brank) means "naked gill": unlike most marine animals, its gills are located outside instead of inside its body. Nudibranchs come in many different sizes and shapes and are often patterned in brilliant colors. This one is about one foot long and belongs to one of the largest species. It sways through the water like a belly dancer. Other species are only a few inches in length and creep slowly across the reef. Nudibranchs feed on sponges, algae, and anemones.

**Nudibranch**   Red Sea, Sinai Peninsula, Egypt

# This tiny Octopus has a very venomous bite.

Although it is only the size of your fist, this tiny blue-ringed octopus has a very venomous bite. Octopuses have eight arms (*octo* means "eight" in Latin) with a beak in the center. They feed on fish and shellfish. Octopuses have no bones and can squeeze and stretch themselves to fit into cracks and holes on the bottom. They can change color, camouflage themselves, and hide themselves in a cloud of ink. They get oxygen by drawing water through a siphon, which is like a small hose, visible in this photograph just beneath the octopus's eye. When they need to move quickly to escape danger, as this one is doing, octopuses force water out of their siphons and jet away.

**Blue-ringed octopus**
Great Australian Bight, Australia

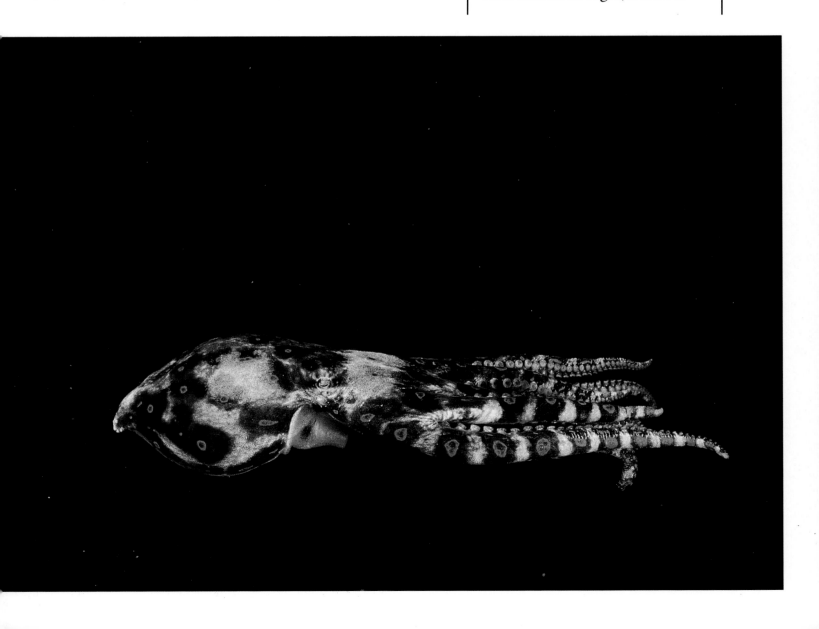

# P

Filled with water, these Pufferfish are impossible for other fish to swallow.

When danger threatens, spiny pufferfish fill themselves with water. Inflated, they are about the size of a soccer ball. Their pointed, porcupine-like spines stick out, making it impossible for other fish to eat them. Pufferfish have sharp, beaklike mouths, which they use to crunch up shellfish such as clams and mussels. They also eat sea urchins and crabs. There are many different species of pufferfish throughout the world. Some are only a few inches long; others grow to two or three feet. Most do not have sharp spines like these, but many are poisonous to eat.

**Spiny pufferfish**   Red Sea, Sinai Peninsula, Egypt

**Queen angelfish**   Caribbean Sea, Cayman Islands

Brilliantly and royally colored, the queen angelfish is one of the most beautiful of the many kinds of fish that live on the coral reefs of the Caribbean Sea. There are many species of angelfish, including the gray angelfish and the yellow and black French angelfish, but none is as distinctly colored as the queen angelfish. The colorful markings may enable the angelfish to recognize other members of the same species in order to mate. Angelfish eat mostly sponges and grow to over one foot long.

# The Queen Angelfish is one of the most beautiful fish on the reef.

# This Red Irish Lord is perfectly camouflaged.

R

**Red Irish lord**   Pacific Ocean, British Columbia

Despite its fantastic colors, the red Irish lord blends in perfectly with its surroundings. It lives in the North Pacific Ocean off the coasts of Canada and the United States. This clear, cold water sea is as colorful as a tropical reef: the rocks and the sea bottom are covered with brilliantly colored anemones, sponges, and soft corals. Cool ocean currents bring in a rich broth of plankton that provides food for many species of marine life. The red Irish lord waits patiently, watching with its large, sensitive eyes for its prey—other small fish. This one was so sure of its camouflage that it was possible for a diver to touch it and even pick it up before it moved a fin.

# S

The Australian sea lion is among the friendliest of all sea lions. This one lives in a colony on an island called Hopkins Island. When divers approach, the sea lions dive into the water, play with them, and chew on their swim fins. Australian sea lions are small for sea lions, less than six feet long, and blond in color. Sea lions are mammals. They must come to the surface to breathe air but can hold their breath underwater for a long time, up to thirty minutes. At night sea lions go far out to sea to hunt fish and squid. During the day they lie on the rocks, basking in the sun.

**Australian sea lion**
Great Australian Bight, Australia

## Sea Lions can hold their breath for up to thirty minutes.

**Hawksbill turtle**   Atlantic Ocean, Bahamas

This hawksbill turtle glides through the water using its large flippers like underwater wings. Hawksbills breathe air, as do all species of turtle, and lay their eggs on sandy beaches. They eat fish and jellyfish and graze on sea grass. Hawksbill turtles are found in warm, tropical seas all over the world. Their shells are the most beautiful of all turtle shells and are used for making tortoiseshell jewelry. Because of this, people have hunted hawksbill turtles so much that there are very few left. They are on the endangered species list, and in many countries it is now against the law to catch them. It is also against the law to bring any hawksbill turtle-shell jewelry into the United States.

# This Turtle glides through the water using its flippers like wings.

T

# The Unicorn Fish has a single horn on its head.

**Unicorn fish** Red Sea, Sinai Peninsula, Egypt

The unicorn fish has a single horn on its head, just like the mythical land unicorn. Unicorn fish live on the coral reefs of the Pacific Ocean, the Indian Ocean, and the Red Sea. They sometimes swim in great schools at the edge of the reef, where the current is strong and rich in the plankton they like to eat; at other times they graze on the algae that cover the corals of the reef. No one is sure what the horn is for, but it may be used for fighting. This unicorn fish has scars that may be from fighting with other unicorn fish.

# The Venus Tuskfish uses its tusks for hunting shellfish.

## V

**Venus tuskfish**  Pacific Ocean, Great Barrier Reef, Australia

The Venus tuskfish has four long tusks that stick out of its mouth—two on the top and two on the bottom. Inside its mouth are wonderfully strong shorter teeth. The tusks are used for hunting in the sand for food such as shrimps or crabs, and for breaking apart clams, scallops, and sea urchins. The teeth inside the mouth grind up these nutritious meals. The tusks are also used in nest building to move about rocks and bits of coral. On the reef the Venus tuskfish seems to be constantly working. It is always busy digging, gnawing, eating, and guarding its territory.

# W

## The Whale Shark is the largest shark in the sea.

The whale shark is not a whale but a shark; in fact, it is the largest species of shark in the sea. This one is over forty feet long—the largest ever photographed. Although they have thousands of tiny teeth, they are not dangerous to divers. They feed on plankton and small fish, which they catch by swimming through the ocean with their huge mouths wide open. Water is forced down their throats, and strainers and gill rakers strain out the food; the water is then flushed out through the whale shark's gills. Schools of pilotfish swim with this great creature, and remoras, or suckerfish, hang on to it near its jaws.

**Whale shark**   Gulf of California, Baja, Mexico

# X marks the spot!

**Treasure hunt**  Gulf of Mexico, Florida

A diver makes an exciting find during a treasure-salvaging expedition: a 300-year-old gold bar from the wreck of the Spanish ship *Atocha,* which sank in 1622 in a hurricane off the Florida Keys. Gold never changes color or becomes covered with marine growth when it is underwater. It stays as bright as the day it came from the mint. On old maps, mapmakers would put an "X" where they thought treasure ships sank. Modern treasure hunters must begin by examining old records and maps to try and discover where ships were lost. Then divers begin carefully searching the sea bottom. It took more than twenty years to discover and salvage the treasure from the *Atocha.*

# Yellow-Headed Jawfish are constantly digging and building.

Yellow-headed jawfish build their homes in the rocky bottom of the Caribbean Sea. Although they are less than four inches long, jawfish have very strong jaws, and they carefully construct their burrows by wedging and bracing pebbles together. They can pick up large rocks that fall down their holes and are constantly rebuilding, cleaning, and digging. To feed, the jawfish hovers over its burrow waving its fins gently, then darts toward a drifting piece of plankton. When danger approaches, it dives directly back into its hole—sometimes headfirst, sometimes tailfirst. The yellow-headed jawfish is a mouth brooder, which means that the father takes care of the young by holding them in his mouth. When he has to feed himself, he spits the young into the burrow for a moment.

**Yellow-headed jawfish**
Caribbean Sea, Cayman Islands

# The Zebrafish has thirteen deadly poisonous spines.

## Z

**Zebrafish**   Red Sea,
Sinai Peninsula, Egypt

The zebrafish is protected from predators by thirteen poisonous spines along its back. Touching these spines can cause intense pain and even death. But it is one of the most beautiful fish in the sea, looking like a floating flower. The zebrafish uses its feather-like fins to hover slowly in the water and sweep little fish into its mouth. At night it hovers on the reef as if imitating coral sea fans gently moving in the current, then darts quickly forward to catch its prey. Zebrafish have been known to hunt in groups, working together and herding schools of smaller fish toward each other's mouths. They also eat tiny shrimps. Sometimes called the lionfish, turkeyfish, or, in Australia, the butterfly cod, the zebrafish grows to about eighteen inches in length.

# glossary

**Algae** Small plants that live in water. They have no flowers, leaves, stems, or roots, but like other plants they need sunlight to grow.

**Coral** A small animal related to jellyfish and anemones. Corals have no internal skeleton, but some species (known as "hard" corals) form hard, rocklike external skeletons. These  skeletons remain after the animal itself is dead; over hundreds of years, millions of them can build up to form a *coral reef.*

**Coral reef** An underwater structure built from millions of hard or "reef building" corals. There are three kinds of coral reef: **fringing reefs,** which are attached to the shore; **barrier reefs** (such as Australia's Great Barrier Reef), which are separated from the shore but parallel to it; and **atolls,** which are circular coral reefs surrounding a lagoon.

**Crustacean** An animal with no backbone and a shell-like external skeleton. Most crustaceans live in water; they include shrimps, lobsters, and crabs.

**Endangered species** An animal that is threatened with extinction, often because of overhunting or the destruction of its habitat by humans.

**Fin** A winglike attachment to fish and other underwater animals that provides movement and balance. There are two sorts of  fin: *paired* fins (in twos, one on each side of the body) and *median* fins (a single fin running along the body). Paired fins include the **pectoral fins,** which are positioned at the front and underneath the animal. Median fins include the **dorsal fin,** a vertical fin along the animal's back.

**Gill** The organ in a fish or other underwater creature that extracts oxygen from the water and enables the animal to "breathe."

**Mammal** A warm-blooded, air-breathing animal that feeds its young on milk. Ocean-dwelling mammals include seals, sea lions,  dolphins, manatees, and whales. They do not have gills and must come to the surface regularly to breathe.

**Plankton** Microscopic plants and animals that drift in the ocean currents and provide food for larger sea animals. *Plankton* is a Greek word meaning "wanderer" or "drifter." Plants are called **phytoplankton** and animals are called **zooplankton.**

**Predator** An animal that survives by catching and eating other animals.

# *taking pictures underwater*

Taking pictures underwater requires a lot of equipment and good teamwork. Different fish and different pictures need different equipment, and you can't change camera lenses or film underwater. On most dives, we take eight to ten cameras fitted with different lenses and lights. Each camera weighs about twenty-five pounds on the surface; underwater they weigh about two pounds. We work together to prepare all the equipment before every dive. While underwater we often help each other by carrying cameras, positioning lights, or attracting fish.

Most cameras are put in waterproof cases called underwater housings. These are

made of aluminum, and the photographer can work all the camera's controls from the outside. There are special dome ports for the wide angle lenses and long ports for the telephoto lenses. The ports are attached to the front of the housings.

The underwater world is blue, so many photographs require artificial light to show the brilliant colors of their subjects. Special underwater electronic flashes do this job. The flashes—called strobes—are attached to the camera housings with aluminum arms. These arms have joints that can bend and turn so the lights can be aimed at the subject at different angles.

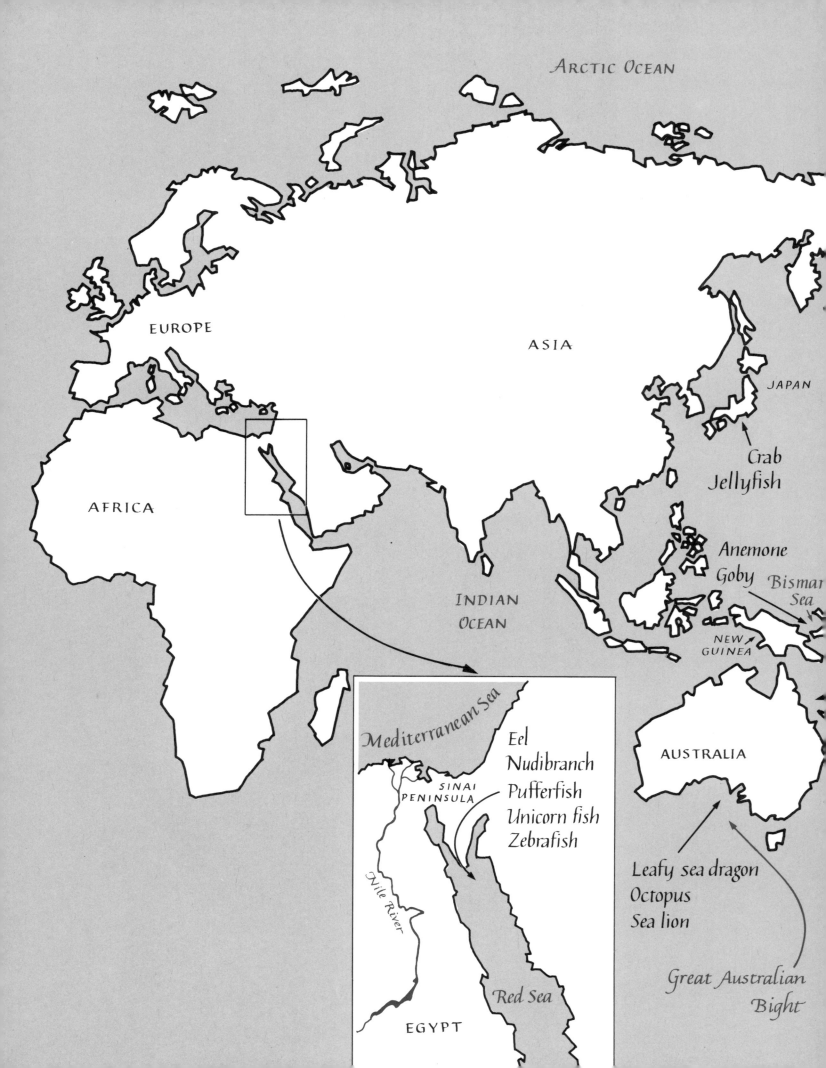

ARCTIC OCEAN

EUROPE

ASIA

JAPAN

Crab
Jellyfish

AFRICA

Anemone
Goby

Bismar
Sea

INDIAN
OCEAN

NEW
GUINEA

AUSTRALIA

Mediterranean Sea

Eel
Nudibranch
Pufferfish
Unicorn fish
Zebrafish

SINAI
PENINSULA

Leafy sea dragon
Octopus
Sea lion

Nile River

Red Sea

Great Australian
Bight

EGYPT